Constant State
of Love

Constant State of Love

Anran Liken

To order additional copies of this book, contact:
Xlibris
UK TFN: 0800 0148620 (Toll Free inside the UK)
UK Local: 02036 956328 (+44 20 3695 6328 from outside the UK)
www.Xlibrispublishing.co.uk
Orders@Xlibrispublishing.co.uk
814071

Contents

Angel With In

You look at me and see an angel
Hoping for things that angels bring
Inside when you look deeper
you find a woman screaming out for love
The challenge, you take up
find the truth break in to claim
what is waiting there for you
A heart full of love with much to spare
for all who take challenge to seek the truth within

Breath Of Giving

You came when need a breath of air
Your fine words temptingly glorious
Never would you see the love inside

A star from afar reaching down in time
A hand of friendship gift from heaven
Gods be seen gods be here

Miles apart oceans in between
Never dreams drowning in the seas
Loves request love be gone

Dreams coming down wind steps
Swirling tempting lushly
Never lifting never loving

Always give always wanting
Never having never keeping
Giving love loosing love

Chances

One moment in time can change a life
Seconds change a moment into a chance
it is a look, a word, a touch of a hand, melding of minds
Twining of hands of beating hearts loving each
other from far of lands
Oceans in between chances of waves reach
for the stars
Moon lite sparkles as tears fall down from the
clouds as chances missed
Laughter sprinkles hope into the cracks
bringing chances shimmering to life new
growth of hope

Crashing

Waves crashing rolling onto empty beaches
Willing asking 'when will we play again
Tides turning day after day waiting

For little footprints laughing giggling chasing
Running
Blankets laid food is set handprints in the sand
returning for feast

Lovers turning towards each other
water tickling toes, sand holding together
Dreams echoes of what use to be,
dreams of what can come to pass

Trickling back footprints in the sand
waves trailing over soft feet
Little fingers playing building castles
waves washing away remainder of dreams

Footprints

Our life is but never knowing
how long we have left
people come in 'n' out of your life leaving
footprints across our hearts
just like footprints in the sand

Some good memories, bad, ugly, and some
great memories, awesome memories,
but the ones that seem to leave the most is
our sad memories
We try to leave these behind sometimes
those outweigh all other memories

You came and left more than footprints
you took hold of a heart
Slowly ever so slowly it is healing
With the footprints you left so lovingly behind
Holding a heart ever so gently

Tides will change washing footprints away
but footprints left in a heart are there for life
keeping memories lovingly safe for all of time

Garden Of Dreams

Sat in my garden listening to birds fighting
over food
My eyes are closed lifting up to the sun rising
Feeling it on my face warming with each stroke
passing across like a hand caressing
Cup of tea in hand coffee waiting for you to join
Your hand strokes across my hair caressing as
you sit beside me
Rolling down my arm to hold of hands
taking your coffee cup
eyes open smile upon my face dreaming just again
sat in my garden listening to birds fighting over food

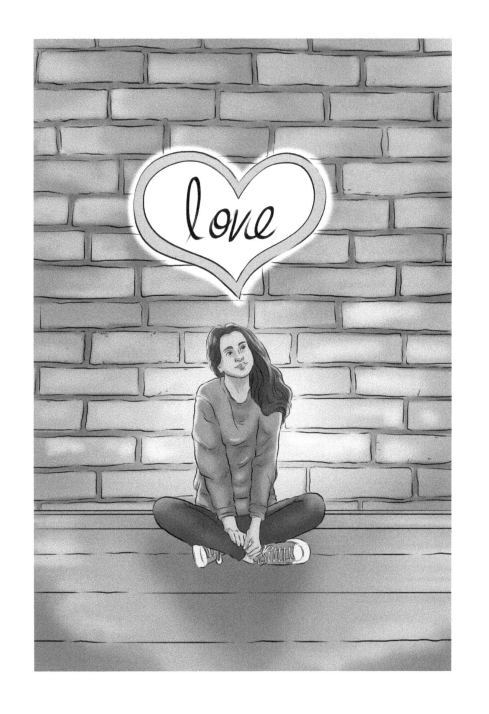

Heart And Head

I fall to sleep you are in my heart my head
I do not know if I dream of you
I do know I awake you are in my heart my head

Circling round 'n' round giving me hope giving me love
Missing you more with each passing day
Passing hour passing minute seconds

Wanting longing for your touch wanting longing to touch you
Running fingers over your chest threw your hair
feeling soft gentle skin soft hair tickling
my fingertips hard muscle
I fall to sleep you are in my heart you are in my head

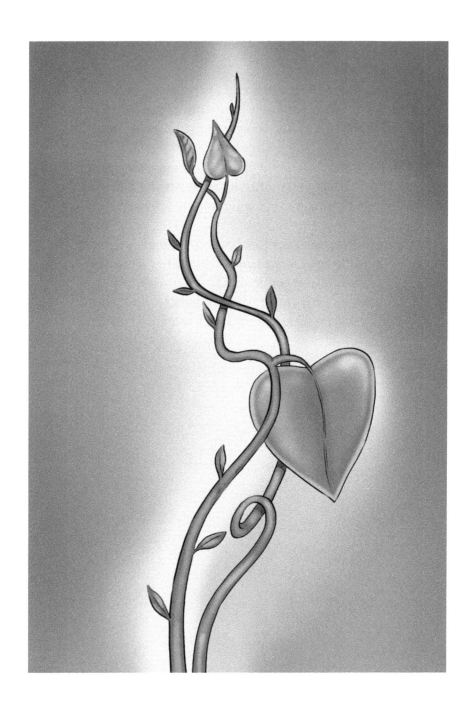

Heart Grows Fonder

Saw you from afar my heart knew you in an instant
My mind whispering not a chance
Watch you from other side never knowing the
Love coming to you
Hurting so much the heart almost burst with wanting
Stop watching, hoping it will stop this loving
You creep more and deeply into
my heart hiding in every empty hole
Giving in to watch once more laughing at your jokes
Crying knowing that neve will i ever get to touch you hold you
Once more stop must stop hurting too much
Then hope you say HI
Ever hoping, needing, loving, wanting to tell
No must not, keep secret just for me
She didn't, she wanted to be out she burst
Through shouting so that the heavens could hear

Knowing

Wind blowing through sea crashing on the shore breaking
spray wet air taste of sea salt on lips caressing with thy tongue
Sea birds crying diving down catching of fish fighting
over the lucky ones pinching of bits wanting more
People walking, dogs playing chasing toys jumping into
waves rolling onto the beach talking to other dogs
Surfers catching waves falling into seas not landing right catch
the next see how it goes falling until that sweet one arrives
He's watching checking can't see her she must be, is that her
hair blowing in the wind always fighting to keep it tamed
Smiling at her walking towards him does she see me yet,
no, then she feels him watching her looks up smiles
Hearts jumping for both knowing you are with him,
her for the right reasons you complete each other

Light That Shines

You are the light that shines so brightly in her heart
So precious is the heart beating time and time again
Gently with your hand you hold the gem of life her life

She shines when you are near so brightly that she blinds you
She shows you love for you by giving you her heart
So gently does it taking hold of your heart caressing it till it calms
Holding it close till your two hearts beating as one
coming together so they beat in unison

Blending as one reaching for the light that shines
so brightly with love never ending feeding the light,
so, she shines brighter with every tender moment,
every word, every touch, kiss, caress
Leading to the light that shines ever brighter

Lyrical Words

Words musical lyrics sing to us speaking
differently to each and everyone

Words saying what we want need to hear
telling tales

Music sings the tune that plays to our strings
pulling on each and everyone

Lyrics that fill in with music playing on the
strings that pass through our body playing on
all of them

We know not what they feel we know not what
they make
Expression of love anger pain sorrow sadness

Each and everyone feels something differently
taking us to different places different times
different presences

Pulling more and more drawing us in deeper
and deeper we fall into the pool of
musical word lyrical

Mirrors

Rising in the morning looking out to see light reflecting
back at you looking out of mirrors to see if
life changes but nothing lifted she is looking back at her
she sees her but doesn't understand why people see
what they see in her

Angel face, beautiful, cute, is what they say but what some see
butter wouldn't melt in her mouth; all she sees is her normal self
nothing special for she knows her, knows what she is capable of
so much more never allowed to be

Wondering aimlessly around listening watching
helping fixing so others can achieve guiding
through the dark storms she sees in her head
helping to pull her through into the
reflection of herself seeing into mirrors

Looking into the eyes of others she sees their
pain knows their need helps with all
mirrors of the soul the eyes will be leaving
trails of past streaks across the face of vessels
left behind she sees all how she feels
how she sees mirrors reflection

My Heart So Sings

My heart so sings and
just don't understand why?
When I look upon your face,
tears of joy leak
Down from my face
You became apart of me
in a short time of space
But feelings of knowing
you are given time of place
My heart knows what she wants
Yearning love for a man
Untouchable until now
Being together is all in a cloud
Of soft white sand with
sea lapping at our feet
my heart so sings when looking
upon your face

Mystic dreams

Night comes dreams come out to play
Fairies dragons pixies swirling around in
clouds of dreams
There they are man walking looking got to
find her must have her must protect can't
understand why it as to be her
She passed through the dreams of fairies
dragons and pixies playing laughing
having fun riding on the back of
dragons and horses
He sees her gliding through the clouds
riding majestic creatures fairies playing
with her golden locks
He feels movement burning through him
Can't control what he's sensing pixies
whispering 'go get her she is yours'
mischief mix
She's laughing stops seeing him standing
dragon swoops down circling around him
checking all lowers down she decanters
Walking slowly towards him hands stretched
out holding his eyes sparkling with
wanting lips curved with expectations
You touch lights flash sparks crackle
stepping into each other holding feeling
caressing daring to kiss,
making love never ending
Lips touch breath catches falling deeper
drowning into each other kissing deeper
taking more 'n' more you're the breath
of each other

Your need for breath her need for breath
breathing for each other coming as one
being as one
Fairies pixies and dragons wrapping you in
a cloak of mystery protecting forever
stroking of mist blending together
making as one

Pain

Pain is hard but it is the easiest of all emotions
to hurt the most
We all feel it 'n' hide it in our own way
It comes in definitely descriptions each one
Hurting differently
Injuries in a pain that is instant can take its time
to easy away, rubbing eases inside but never goes
letting you, letting me down is a sadness of
pain, trust, faith, all come with each other
letting go of yourself integrity is priceless
once lost harder to regain
love is a joyous pain circling around
our heart easily broken piece by piece
over time it overwhelms us
it is the first pain you feel in life
pain is part of us, rejoice in it, cry, scream,
is always around running our life
hiding it all the time never letting go

Please Do Not Cry

Please do not cry, or shed a tear
For that, that is me
Is still here with you
In your heart that beats
Everyday for you
In your memories that
Run in rings around your mind
Always remember that
I had everything you are feeling
All the love you
Feel you have lost
It is still there
In every thought
Until we meet again

Return Of Light

You see her glow, feeling that light burning
inside of you shining ever brighter you looking
into her eyes see the mischievous sparkle
shining with love for you

Your heart jumps extra with every look she
gives you every turned-up smile when she
knows you are watching her makes your heart
beat faster

You check for hoping there is something from
her, a cheeky kiss, a beating heart, a note of love,
your breath catches yes there is,
teasing you to answer

No must resist not straight away never answer
but I've been waiting wanting hoping for
something in return to spark the light keeping
it burning, is she the one to return the light

Rivers Or Tears

We know not where they come from
But leak out of our eyes
Pain is cause of which no one can explain
Hearts are broken taken away returned from
Whence they came

Rivers flow like blood of tears trailing down
Faces as rivers on the land carving ways to
Leave the stains of life
Drying strokes wipe away with tender loving care

Trailing kisses taking away pain of hunger
Wanting waiting hoping never receiving
always giving
Rivers of tears leading away taking of love
wanting hoping waiting pain down to where
thy became

Stirring storms bubbling anger keeping silent
Keeping hold to thy self
Lifting higher till a volcano explodes
flooding waters

Pain no more leaking out of every crevasse
can't hold it in any longer needing realise
River of tears flowing away the pain of hurting
wanting waiting needing hoping.

Short Of Life

Our life is but short never knowing how long
we have left
People come in 'n' out of your life leaving
footprints across our hearts
just like footprints in the sand

Some good memories, some great memories,
awesome memories
But the ones that seem to leave the most
are our sad memories
we try to leave these behind sometimes
those outweigh all other memories

You came and left more than footprints
you took hold of a heart
Slowly ever so slowly it is healing
With footprints you left so lovingly behind
holding a heart ever so gently

Tides will change washing footprints away
but footprints left in a heart are there for life
keeping memories lovingly safe for all of time

Sonnet Of Love

We gave an Oath too each other
Not knowing if either one is true
For you I have loved your voice drawing me in
I looked up into your eyes looking at me from
the screen but not seeing me
You reached into the deepest parts of my soul
the soul I thought belong to another

For you looked at a picture saw an angel
looking back
Eyes of deep understanding looking into your
heart knowing how you feel seeing your pain
your yearning to be loved for just a man and
not the star that you are but the boy still inside

Every time I heard your voice or saw your face
I was in pain knowing I could never touch
but only look and listen, so I stopped,
yet the yearning was too strong had to watch
just to feel that surge of love to feel alive

You talk to each other like old friends from
long ago both yearning for the
same things just to be loved for you and not
for what you can do for others wanting that
feeling of belonging

Looking at your picture brings a burning
yearning of love in the heart
exciting butterflies flutter around wafting the
flames higher making the feelings stronger
turning in on themselves with tears of joy
when will this yearning quench the love

Your yearning grows stronger for a woman
you're not sure of
she reaches into your soul understanding you
knowing how your wanting to feel, wanting to
be loved just as a man

The doubts maybe real when far from here till
together we shall meet brushing away the
fears and tears stroking of cheeks caressing
each other holding kissing making it all for real
doubts drifting away fear moving letting love
blossom even before it as begun to bloom

Tears

Tears run down my face
Fearful of how I feel
Afraid to believe that this could be real

Heart beating bleeding pain
Shame of thinkin feeling hoping
There might be another chance for you to be loved

Loving in return needing wanting holding
His heart beating by my heart as one together
Blending merging as one beating heart

Tears run down my face
Loving how we feel
Believing that this is for real

Warm Glow Of Love

Sun comes up morning after morning bringing
new hope new life new expectations
Shinning on all that is reachable giving warmth
caressing each molecular of velvet petals
blade of grass reaching each and everyone

Except the deepest dark depths where no light
can reach 'n' only sorrow misery pain dwell
waiting for its next victim but whom shall it be
yes, it can anyone who is out there

There you are warm glow of sunlight on your
face happy smile body lighting with first spark
of hope there is our victim lets go play oh look
there is the first tear

You hold onto your breast as the pain is so
great in your body you start to fall as the
sorrow is so great the misery of seeing what
you are looking at you can't take anymore

But wait what is that light creeping through it
is the soft glow of sunlight but no it is the hand
of love coming to pull you out of the deepest
dark depths of hell

Sun comes caressing over each molecular of
face stroking smiles back reaching all the way
up to your eyes saying it is time to move
forward not looking back let it rest let it be

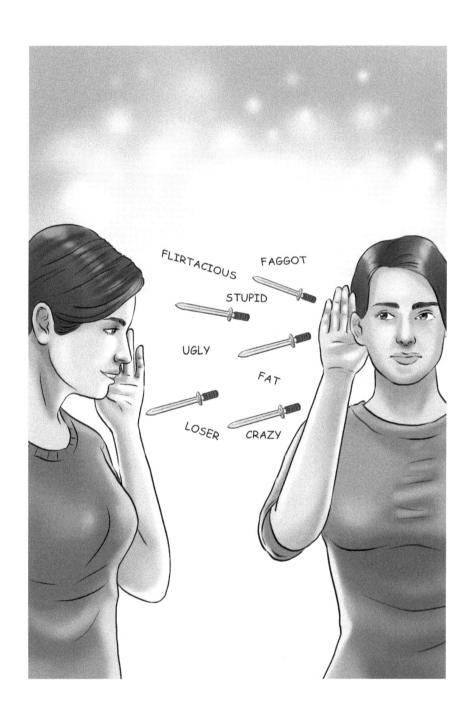

Words Are Swords

Words are swords they can give hope
Happiness, love, make you feel proud with one word
Take away all emotions with the wrong words
sadness, sorrow, heartbreak, devastation, loss
swords are words they can wound, maim, cut,
make you bleed all with a sway of the blade
giving emotional pain with one push of the
blade ending the sadness, sorrow, devastation
of loss
finishing the heartbreak laid in the arms of the
one you love, understanding now thy meaning
of 'words are like swords'

Yearning

You came to me through the screen
I looked into your eyes and I was lost
My heart was beating Hard I thought
it was going to burst out of my body

I cannot remember what I was watching
but I knew from that day on
I could not watch you on the screen again
for hell it was going to be for me

To watch you and not being able to touch
you to tell you how I felt afraid that others
might see what I felt

I tried so many times to watch had too because
family wanted to watch
but for me it was like living in hell

Then I was by myself yet again and there
you were on my screen saving the world
this time I could not hold back anymore

I cried myself to sleep that night knowing
I could never ever kiss you, hold you,
or tell you how I felt

You Know Him

You know he's there
you feel him in here
Heart pounding
every time you think of him
Reading what he's put
hope it is the truth
never really believing
that this spectacular thing
could happen to you
no never is this happening too
you nothing good ever does
just maybe for once believe
that God will let this be for you
you are being give a miracle a gift

Beating Heart Of Love

You light the way in my dark,
your love is the beacon that
I look for in the night
I follow my heart that beats
with every breath you take
I need to hold you close
to look into your eyes and
tell you I'm in love with you
to tell you that I see you,
you that which is the real you
for you are my soulmate
whose heart that beats with my heart
the rhythm blending together
as one beating heart
I love you
I am in love with you
you are my soul
if you are not in this world
I have nothing left to live for
You are the one I want to grow old with
the one I want to share my family with
I give my heart willingly to you
without any conditions it is yours
to do what you must with it
all I ask is that you live

Bittersweet

You brought the sun back into her heart were
only darkness seemed to live, churning of pain
bitter sweetness

Missed beats of music playing never dancing
only burden of faults beating inside the brain,
spark of light catching hold

Lifting movements songs remembering of why
you should be living looking at,
out into the light holding your hand
pulling you to dance

Music flowing freely
dancing in the light of sun rays
flashing in the sky moving closer
holding light with careful hands

Brightnes 'N' Light

Light is dimming clouds closing in,
sunlight dropping below trees,
what will it be tonight,
bats flying, foxes crying,
badgers scurrying through the woodland
That's when it starts the calling the screaming,
pain in your heart aching
crawling at your wall trying to get out
banishing passed the memories
Memories of joy, love, children, grandchildren
all taken away by lies, cheating,
half-truths hiding always afraid to speak out,
memories turn to pain
Beacon of light pushing through the darkness
reaching for your hand, giving hope
where there was non gently pulling
towards beating heart
Slowly lowering of head arms coming around
holding you so tightly helping the memories
bring back joy into the once broken heart
calmly now beating back in time

Game Face

Right here we are got out of the car
bag over shoulder 'click, click, click' goes the cameras
'over here, no over here, oh can I have a selfie,
can I have your autograph
Remembering these are my fans
my bread and butter
putting smile on face
but never reaches my eyes
yeah, yeah, no problems,
okay just here,
right I've got to go folks
Walking away smile gone from my face
thinking dwelling on it all,
do I want to do this till I can't walk no more?
I'm lonely no I want a woman to love me,
me on the inside not what my fans see
Is she out there waiting somewhere hiding?
from me will she be looking for me too
when will meet?
look a message 'very pensive'
interesting no don't message back but,
but what if

Heart

You came into my life and stayed
you never left my heart
you found a hole and hid inside
you made contact
I don't know what to believe anymore is it him
or is it someone playing at being him
I took a leap of faith
believing my heart would n
ever lie to me, she as stayed steady
throughout it all
never given up
but being pushed further
than expected giving everything
that you have
always wanting more

Hope

I look into your eyes
I am drowning in your soul
Your voice is like honey
Tickling down my spine
Your sweet words caring nature
Building hope of love and life
You came out nowhere when I was
Drowning in pain
You were the gift of hope in dark waters
Swirling pulling down deeper and deeper
The star of light shining the way of living
You opened a heart, a heart so lost
A heart in pain, a heart that gave up on love
That gave up on life itself
One simple word is all it took
To open a door for a heart broken
Helping to forget
Giving hope of friendship
Turning into more
Few weeks of words
Laughing teasing
Like old friends coming together
Moments, minutes seem like years
Lost in time for ever real

Lost

Another airport different car park
same people all waiting,
waiting for someone to come
rushing through the doors arms
open wide love radiating out of them
Except her she leans watching everyone else
looking into their hearts feeling their emotions,
some with excitement, some with love, others
thinking what are we going to get this time
There he is, he doesn't see her he is too
focused on the woman he is walking out with
holding hand's, he kisses her a long drawn out kiss
telling her he doesn't want to leave her
She watches the woman walk away
all the while screaming inside 'why' why,
does she always have to go through this
every time why she puts up with this
Smile on her face she steps out to meet him
look of fear on his face, she knows what he is
thinking 'did she see does she know' he
reaches to kiss his wife but she turns away
Walking to the car park talking as though
everything is okay but inside she knows she
needs to break away from all of this or
she will go insane loose her mind
Then it changes he is gone lost forever she is
free but lost, doesn't know what to do
they think she should mourn forever
But he never mourned them, he gave up on them
said goodbye, but would never let her go
she had to stay, if he didn't want her
no else would or could have her

Lost Dreams

Dreams swirling around, sleeping restlessly,
reaching fingertips almost touching just not there,
tears fall down cheeks knowing it will always be this way

Waking with a start feeling sure you had been
touched by his hand, but no it was just a dream,
dream of hoping, but skin still tingling where he caressed

Night after night the same dream,
reaching but loosing never touching,
more restless sleep,
eyes betraying emotions dark shadows appear,
loosing all

Eyes opening feeling reaching out,
smiling face looking into face watching you sleeping,
caresses your face stroking you fully awake
whispering your name both saying
'I love you'

Minute Is All It Takes

We wait for a lifetime but only a minute
'tis all it takes for love to come flooding in
rooms apart a look is all it takes,
a turned-up smile, turn of a head catch of an eye
People call hands touching all ignored
must reach this angel nymph you've been watching
for she does not see you, yet she feels you,
feels you watching senses you walking forward
Room falls silent she turns to you watching you
advance stepping to meet you
touching her face soft as silk
eyes never leaving each other's
Holding her face within your hands
you want her there in the room,
noise of people inches into your mind
she realises where you both are
move round others taking her hand leading of
You're alone together her lips so inviting
she chews on the corner uncertain of what might be,
you reach for her drinking her in touching of lips
gently at first stars crackling with every caress
Plunging deeper taking not caring just needing
must have, lifting up holding getting closer and closer
she takes hold of your face reaching for your lips
breathing you in taking you deeper
Fire burst her glow getting brighter and brighter
for a star you have stolen
a heart of gold will shine with love ever more

Money

Money is all out there diamonds,
rubies, emeralds, garnets, gold, paper, metal coins
we all need it, others greed for it
thinking we are rich from certain countries
When we are the poor ones,
we who have lost what makes us rich,
family friends food on our table due to hard work
a heart that is giving is rich, rich with happiness
Bills get paid with money
entertainment, clothes, other stuff,
but we are rich we are empty
because we no happiness in our hearts
Hearts that are happy
these are the rich ones people
only a happy heart can be rich in life

Needing

I awake hope for a smile,
but nothing not a kiss,
smile, hug, spanking
or beating heart
I miss you so,
distance is my lover,
dreams my companion
Want your touch,
feel of your hand,
caress of your lips
upon my skin
Warm bodies
side by side
holding on never
wanting to let go
Days, hours, minutes,
a week is never enough
needing more time
leading into yearning
for bodies to lay by each other
for ever more a
lifetime will never be enough,
Never enough

Nothing

Heart is bleeding pushing around pumping beating
Fighting all the time to keep alive is it, is this the time
Getting what was wanted just this once, for this once
But no, not meant to be, yet again, not worthy enough
Worthless always feeling worthless, made to feel like nothing
When will the time come, for it to be time to have?
What would make it worth being alive, making it all worth living
Nothing, because that is all you are nothing to anyone and everyone
All you are wanted for is what you can
give, what you have always given
Love was never meant for you, for you are so unlovable
That no man can or would ever love you
Just this once can I have the love before I die

Emptyness

You were brought into my life,
my heart oh so empty,
for my diesel had been taken,
poisoned by bad
You replaced his empty hole
that was getting bigger each day,
you curled into my shoulder
loved me more than any other
We had so many fun times together,
now all of a sudden
it is your time to say goodbye,
you are not in pain,
but you are poorly
My heart is breaking all over again,
that hole as returned
but bigger and emptier than before,
no more cuddles curling into my shoulders

Loneliness

Loneliness is scary,
being and feeling alone
hard to comprehend
a crowded room people
everywhere noise loud talking
smiling drinking
finger food picking
head talking 'need to get out
need to escape'
need to be alone
somewhere quiet
looking for the moment
to escape this crowded room
alone at last, breathing deeply,
in, out, in, out, yes better,
what was that,
no don't I need to be alone
just few more minutes,
empty inside lost feelings
burning ball in chest need to
get it out need get rid of this pain,
again, noise creeping in,
movement in corner of eye
no nothing, turning round
there he is stood in front of you,
looking at each other
understanding
the feeling of hiding from others
kindred souls finding each other
burning empty lost feelings
gone in a flash of light
warm glow of opening
wanting to be together

talking to each other
without opening of mouths
minds melding together
loneliness no more
gather of one

Changes

A door closes does not mean the end,
your last adventure as come to an end
that chapter as finished let a new one begin
Door opens a new adventure to take up
an offer, build a new chapter
leading the way walking through
your fear moving forward
Life is full of changes some we fear,
some we embrace,
others we want to run away from,
the good, the bad, the ugly,
no matter keep on walking
through the fear
Changes are the regrowth,
new birth, life beginning,
life ending moving forwards
never going back
learning from the past
changes all around

Breaking Heart

Heart breaking is the loudest noise
but silent of all for we feel it in our chest
but our mind hears the tearing of the tissue
it is the punching of a boxer hitting your chest
and pushing your heart back through
your body and out of you,
you can hear your body crying
out for it to return but no matter
how loud you scream it is
gone for ever more waiting till the one
who will repair the broken tissue?
stitching it back together
healing the scars taking away
the ache and pain
bring light back to shine

Loving You

I love you more than I can explain,
your mind, your voice, your smile,
your face,
my focus heart can feel words
from songs speak for me
which one to choose for there are so many
each with different ways to say I love you
but non just saying how I want it to be

Reaching into my heart and mind
the words will not come to be,
but maybe I can show you with my kisses,
caress of my hand, hand on your chest
feeling your beating heart
quickening at my touch,
resting my head upon your heart
hearing it beating with everything
that I do with you
everything that I do for you
I love you more than life itself
more than my life is worth

Moon rising touching earth with soft glow
of loving light
cannot show how I dwell on you with my love
wanting to feel you touch the most sacred
part of me
while i caress that,
that is your most sacred part
of you loving you
The way I do hoping to charm you into
loving me the same as I do you and
always would my love

Always Wanting More

Stroking of hair caressing of skin feeling
the shiver tingling down through your bodies
touching breathing in each other

Looking into each other's eyes finding
the truth reaching for the moon and
finding the stars

Gently reaching sliding hands over silky skin
hers reaching touching holding feeling you
tremble tending of strength in muscle

Kissing of body caressing of nipples licking
kissing down structured muscle reaching for you
taking hold gently rubbing sliding playing lips
getting closer catching of breath

Breathing deeper closer and closer
tongue reaching out slicing across your top,
lips closing around you taking you deeper and deeper
moving slowly down you holding cupping

You can't take more turning you caress kissing
stroking down her deep into your mouth
hold breast breathing in her scent

Reaching down deeper you find her she looks
into your eyes both knowing hoping for more
moving further down you reach what is her
you kiss sliding of tongue her soft cries
pushing you deeper

Wanting more tasting her trying to get closer
not enough never enough kiss back up bodies
looking into each other entering slowly
feeling each other, her holding tightly
around you with each thrust

Growing wilder and wilder wanting more
of each other, never reaching always
searching, once is never enough

Will never be enough wanting craving more
bodies depleted yet more is all that it
will ever be always wanting more.

Connection Lost

Breaking heart beating slowly feeling
the connection separate, lost for ever
desperately trying to fix no longer meant to be
like a punch through the chest
grabbing hold and tearing apart
love once so pure

Pushing out through thy body the love
connection lost begone
always searching trying to find
never reaching just missing
gone to pass looking feeling
never be the same wanting
wondering if one should
just walk away

But never, no, that is not the given, fighting for
but must walk away to save ones sanity
life is never the same with a broken heart
you are on the outside wanting to get back in
never understanding this feeling of emptiness,
loneliness, out of time with everything floating
around you not quite in there
not belonging anymore

Lightning Source UK Ltd.
Milton Keynes UK
UKHW010646190421
382245UK00001B/105